NOT ALL
GRANNIES KNIT

NOT ALL GRANNIES KNIT

HOW TO BE A BAD GRANDMOTHER

Joan Pritchett

MICHAEL O'MARA BOOKS LIMITED

First published in Great Britain in 2006 by
Michael O'Mara Books Limited
9 Lion Yard, Tremadoc Road, London SW4 7NQ

A CIP catalogue record for this book is available from the British Library

ISBN (10 digit): 1-84317-209-7

ISBN (13 digit): 978-1-84317-209-3

1 3 5 7 9 10 8 6 4 2

www.mombooks.com

Designed and typeset by Martin Bristow

Illustrations by Judy Brown

Printed and bound in Slovenia by Printing House MKT print d.d.
by arrangement with Korotan, Ljubljana

For all my grandchildren

CONTENTS

Contents

INTRODUCTION

Becoming a grandmother is a strange experience. One minute you're a busy, youthful person getting on with life, and the next minute, WHOOSH! You're one of the older generation.

Did anyone ask *you* how you would feel about this? Did anyone ask you if you were ready to be a grandmother? I don't think so. You don't often hear couples saying 'We're trying for a grandchild.'

You may not *feel* any different, and of course you're *not* any different, but your identity has changed in the eyes of the world. It is one of those events in life (like being born, I suppose) where you have no right of refusal. If only you could say, 'I'm a bit busy now. Could we do this later?' But you can't.

Try to get that sucked-lemon look off your face. Try not to imagine your future painted entirely in varying shades of grey. This is the time for some clear thinking and decisive action.

Being a grandmother does not come with a book of instructions. Although you may feel as if you had just been press-ganged into taking a voyage in a leaking boat, it is essential to try to steer things round to suit yourself as much as possible.

Here are a few interesting thoughts on damage limitation, from one who knows.

CHAPTER ONE

HEARING THE NEWS

It could happen that one day your daughter invites you out to lunch. It strikes you as strange because such an invitation comes once in a blue moon. What on earth could be going on? Perhaps she's hungry.

No, it isn't because she's hungry (although she probably *is* very hungry as it happens), but the reason for the meeting in a public place (where you are obliged to keep your voice down) is to tell you that she is pregnant.

WHAT?

Shh!

And at once, immediately, comes the need for some TACT AND DIPLOMACY. These are probably not things that you normally have to worry about with your daughter, but now they are a must. Look where you are putting your feet, for heaven's sake.

The first words that might spring to mind must not be allowed out of your mouth, because a perfectly understandable response like: 'Oh, my God, you're not are you?' might not go down too well. Keep your wits about you.

Lightning analysis is needed at this crucial moment. The search for clues must begin at once: does the daughter seem pleased about this piece of news – as far as you can tell?

Can you remember your daughter being involved with any particular man in any sort of relationship (e.g. marriage, though not necessarily these days) that might have resulted in this unexpected shocker?

Hearing the News

Not All Grannies Knit

Why is she telling you this?

Is there something she wants you to do?

Is it going to be a nuisance?

Maybe, after all, a hug is the answer. At least hugs give you time to do a bit of mental arithmetic.

Of course, your reaction would be the same if it were your daughter-in-law who had just prematurely aged you. Only in that case you would know for certain that the man involved (i.e. your son) was not ready for fatherhood, which would make the news even more unsettling. You can't expect too much grown-up parenting from someone who still forgets to tie up his shoelaces and walks about with his hair on end, can you?

CHAPTER TWO

THE PREGNANCY

that the pregnancy is considered to be A Good Thing. What can you look forward to for the next six months or so? You can anticipate being told more than you need to know about the health of everyone involved (daily bulletins), and shown dark, incomprehensible pictures of something or other. Although these images are highly prized by the parents, to you they look like satellite weather maps of storms, and sometimes they have an almost other-worldly quality.

Not All Grannies Knit

Pregnancy can be competitive these days – it is something to be proud of, you see. Remember to exude an air of pride as your daughter's bump precedes you, and everyone else, down the street.

But don't waste your time trying to interest the parents-to-be in world wars, tales of top movie stars changing sex, or the price of coffee. During a pregnancy there are no other topics of conversation.

Try not to laugh when the expectant couple come back from their latest antenatal class talking about how BEAUTIFUL natural childbirth is. If you didn't know better, you might get the impression that giving birth to a child was like composing the perfect sonnet or producing an existential work of art – but you *do* know better. Nobody mentions the mess.

While the hormones of the mother-to-be are turning her into a tear-stained bundle of emotions, You are expected to maintain your composure at all times and, if anyone should ask, tell them how proud you are, and how very, very happy. Happy on the scale of Heidi, Pollyanna and Rebecca of Sunnybrook Farm, they must understand.

Thank heavens that nature has put a time limit on pregnancy. Just be glad that your daughter is not a camel (thirteen months) or an opossum (twelve and a half days). A twelve-and-a-half-day pregnancy is a terrifying notion.

CHAPTER THREE

THE NAMING OF NAMES

So, the baby is on its way. Well done. Now, of course, the next most important thing to think about is the name. No, not the child's name; it is what *you* are to be called in your role as grandmother – because that name is going to be with you for the rest of your life, my friend. THE REST OF YOUR LIFE!

That grandmother tag could well feature in your obituary. Or, think about this carefully, be written in flowers and paraded through the streets at your funeral. 'There goes Noony', people will say. 'It's a merciful release really'.

NOONY

Here lies our
sadly departed
NOONY
Gone but not
forgotten
R.I.P.

The worst thing you can do – the absolute 'Let's-go-for-a-sail-on-the-*Titanic*' type of decision – is to leave it until the baby is old enough to make silly noises and come up with a name for you itself. DO NOT DO THIS.

If you find you are introducing yourself at family gatherings for all the years to come with the words, 'Hello, I'm Ga-Ga', you have no one but yourself to blame.

It's the same with those pretty baby-talk names sometimes given to children, which may not always suit a growing girl or boy.

Grandmothers' nerves will be shredded if they end up with the wrong name. Imagine hearing a shriek of 'Gummy, Gummy!' echoing around your favourite store. Think of all the people on the top deck of a bus craning their necks to see what 'Nanny Boobies' looks like . . .

Think of something clever and be quick about it before your daughter or your daughter-in-law or your son (treacherous bastard) comes up with a jokey suggestion that sticks.

If you wanted to go exotic, or European Union, you could toy with, for example, Babka, Avo, Grossmutter, Oma, Yaya, Grootje, Babaanne, and plenty more where they came from.

What can you do with your existing names? Does your surname lend itself to being shortened in any way to something more youthful and more FUN. A friend of mine became known as Toffee because of the sweets she always carried in her bag.

Not such a bad idea, I thought. Or maybe your initials would work better? Perhaps they spell out something amusing and catchy? If they don't, it's your parents' fault. That's another thing you can blame them for – although you probably have more than enough already.

CHAPTER FOUR

NAMING THE CHILD

Ah yes, the moment of truth. This is when you should find out what you'll be expected to call your new grandchild for the rest of its life.

From quite early on in the pregnancy you will be bombarded by a barrage of possible names for the baby. Friends and relations will all want their say and will expect you to support their ludicrous ideas. 'There's some raw work pulled at the font from time to time, is there not?' as P. G. Wodehouse observed.

STAY OUT OF IT.

Your advice will count for nothing. A name definitely agreed upon one day will be tossed out the next. A moment's whim can bring in a flamboyant outsider of a name, just when you thought hunky was dory.

Pregnant young women are prone to passing whims. It is well known that due to their condition they are all a little insane anyway, so a passing whim is nothing to them. (This is all the more noticeable if the young woman in question was half-cracked in the first place.)

Of course, in the Secret Country of your Imagination things are done differently. In that Happy Place your daughter has had the presence of mind to marry a charming young man with a Country Seat. Over afternoon tea under a cedar tree in the grounds, they tell you that should their baby be a girl, it will be named after you as a token of their love and admiration. They are quite adamant about it and will listen to no arguments. You retire, blushing, to play with the peacocks on the croquet lawn.

WAKE UP!

Naming the Child

In reality your daughter is telephoning to ask you which name you prefer if the baby is a girl – Hero or Flavia?

Don't worry. It will be something different tomorrow. Even after the baby is born, a surprisingly long time can pass before a decision has to be made. Stay calm. Stay detached. Stay out of it. You can always call the offspring something different when you come face to face with it.

CHAPTER FIVE

THE BIRTH

As the date of the birth draws near, make sure your social calendar is full of activities. The proper place for a grandmother at the crucial moment is among friends, being entertained to keep her mind off things, and wined and dined to keep her strength up.

But despite taking great pains to be elsewhere and otherwise engaged as the time of delivery approaches, if you haven't the nerve to keep your mobile phone switched off, you are certain to be kept fully informed, make no mistake about it.

First of all, your son-in-law will ring you to tell you that your daughter has gone into labour. That's done it. Remember that sickly discomfort you always get when your daughter has something wrong with her? Yes, it's happening again now, and it's worse than ever. However, the real purpose of the telephone call was to ask you if your daughter has discussed her Birth Plan with you . . .

'What? What birth plan? She's going to have a baby. That's the plan. Didn't anybody tell you?'

He explains that these days women who are expecting babies often draw up a birth plan for themselves – about how they would like to have their baby and the sort of atmosphere they would feel most comfortable in. This can involve music, water, chimes, chanting, candles, and sound effects. His problem is that your daughter had been looking forward to a special compilation of music that they had downloaded together for the occasion . . . and now he can't find her iPod. Do you think she'll mind?

'Just a minute. What's all this about music and candles?
She's not going off to dance round a tree somewhere, is she?'

You can't help him and you can't help yourself. You suggest that
he gets himself to his wife's side with or without the music and
you turn down his kind offer to keep you up to date as things
progress. When push comes to shove you don't really want to
know. Why don't they do all-over epidurals for Grandmothers?
The waiting is almost worse than having the baby yourself.

The Birth

Not All Grannies Knit

After far, far too long, he rings back, but appears to have lost the power of joined-up speech, and all you can gather is that 'a little baby has been born'. There's a lot about his own emotions and contributions to the occasion (not interested), but eventually he remembers to tell you about the baby's weight and wellbeing, and that your daughter is tired, but perfectly fine and very happy.

When you put the telephone down at last, your husband is standing in the middle of the room in his pyjamas, hair on end, peering at you from tiny, middle-of-the-night eyes because he's been asleep for hours. 'Do you think I should open the champagne?' he asks.

'I think a cup of tea might be rather nicer, if you don't mind,' you reply.

As you try to come to terms with the wonderful fact that a whole new person has come into the world, it dawns on you that You Are a Grandmother. Just imagine! What a laugh!

A little voice inside you, who never knows when to shut up, is wondering what asking for a cup of tea on such a momentous occasion might suggest. 'It sounds like the sort of thing a Grandmother would say, don't you think?' your inner friend points out. 'A bit – how can I put this – elderly?'

Never listen to little voices in the night. They have nothing to offer you but tears or pointless anxieties.

Chapter Six

COMING FACE TO FACE WITH IT

I had a friend who fainted the first time she laid eyes on her grandchild. She said at the time that she was overcome with emotion, but confessed to me privately that the emotion she had felt was fear. 'It was big,' she said. 'It was huge . . . and it was a funny colour.'

She had noticed something important there. Babies are bigger these days. Remember to expect BIG.

Coming Face to Face with It

Not All Grannies Knit

Soon after the birth you will be informed that you can pay your first visit – and no, you can't get out of it. You can only hope that they have put away the birthing pool and tidied up generally before you arrive.

You're holding aloft the lilac tree in full bloom that you've just bought from the hospital gift shop. (They ought to be able to open a new ward with the money it cost you.)

As you approach the new mother's bed and notice all those bundled up newborn babies in identical cots, Do Not give them a second glance. You do not know which is the right baby, and if you pick the wrong baby you will never live it down. Wait to be introduced.

At this crucial point, can I offer you a little advice? Having made a mental note not to faint or even yelp, you do have to vocalize some emotion when peering into the cot for the first time. May I suggest mewing? Mewing is the noise you would make if a dear friend was telling you about something really frightful that had happened to them, but you were not really listening. You may need to practise in advance. For some reason a series of mews conveys the right message. It could be Emotional Support or it could be Speechless Admiration – I don't know. But whatever it is, it delivers the goods.

Coming Face to Face with It

Not All Grannies Knit

When the time finally comes for you to have a good look at the baby, you discover that it's wearing a bonnet and mittens (do they come fully dressed these days?) and it's not that big, actually. In fact it looks quite small. Poor little soul. And saddled with such an awful name too.

It is difficult to see the baby properly because it is being loomed over by a dreadful toy rabbit. Apart from being a garish yellow colour, the rabbit also looks like Ken Dodd in a spotted bow tie.

'Isn't that a darling rabbit?' the new mother says. 'That was a present from Granny Jenkins.'

The Other Grandmother! For Heaven's Sake! Has she no shame? Fancy rushing into a hospital at the crack of dawn and filling the place up with rabbits. If she wanted to give the baby some sort of toy, would it not have been more appropriate to knit something herself? Does Granny Jenkins not knit? 'Oh yes, she's a brilliant knitter!' A lime-green matinee jacket is produced, which must never be allowed near the baby.

Your offer of a quick snapshot of the newborn is greeted with the reminder that Granny Jenkins has already been busy with her digital camera, and will soon be heading back to her state-of-the-art computer to shoot off email copies of her efforts to a waiting world.

This is a whole new aspect of grandmotherhood that you had not foreseen. There are two of you. DAMN.

If only they hadn't given the poor child such an embarrassing name, you could retaliate by having the birth commemorated on a plate or woven into a wall hanging. But the idea of an artist or an embroiderer snorting with laughter over their work is enough to put you off that idea.

Do you see what is happening here? You have begun to feel protective towards that small person in the cot. Well, poor thing. It will have a lot to put up with, won't it? Look who it has drawn for parents in the lottery of life, and you know for a fact that they have no idea what they're doing, BECAUSE THEY'VE NEVER DONE IT BEFORE.

CHAPTER SEVEN

HOW DOES IT FEEL TO BE A GRANDMOTHER?

After spending precious minutes with the mother and baby during that first emotional visit, it's time to leave the hospital (still carrying your lilac tree unfortunately, because your daughter didn't think much of it – 'What's that branchy thing?' she asked, giving it a withering look).

In spite of this setback, however, it is a moment to congratulate yourself wholeheartedly. What a triumph this has been for you personally. The family tree has grown a new twig. The future has been secured. The next generation has arrived. And it was hardly any trouble at all!

So how does it feel to be a Grandmother? A lot of people, including your daughter/daughter-in-law/son, as well as people you had thought of as friends, greet you with this idiotic opening line. You'd think people would have a bit more sensitivity at such a time, wouldn't you? But no. Some husbands have even been known to threaten divorce 'because they don't fancy the idea of sleeping with a grandmother'. Oh, how killing! What an absolute hoot!

How Does It Feel to Be a Grandmother?

The truth is, there is no answer to this ridiculous question.
You feel just the same as before, thanks for asking.

'So, you're a grandmother now?' your best friend chortles.
Why is she chortling and what is that gleam in her eye?
You have arrived before she has at one of life's great milestones
and that has made her feel younger and better about herself.
Your new status has not changed you in any way, however,
and she knows it, but that does not spoil her enjoyment of it all.

CHAPTER EIGHT

THE IMMEDIATE FUTURE

Following the euphoria you felt when leaving the hospital after your first encounter with the newborn, there is plenty to bring you right back down to earth. Including the telephone calls from old acquaintances and distant family members, people with whom you sincerely hoped you had lost touch. But no, here they are, all ringing up to say they don't like the baby's name. And you have to ring them all back and pretend you *do* like the baby's name, which takes a lot of graciousness and good acting.

'Well, they're not coming to the christening for a start,' may well be your reaction as you put down the phone.

At this stage, however, you don't really know if there's even going to be a christening or some other kind of naming ceremony, but whatever it is, you are going to be there, ready to rugby tackle Granny Jenkins if she tries any of her technical wizardry on you.

Of course, if it does turn out to be one of the more traditional types of christenings, there is a chance that the baby may be in need of a long, white robe and a big, lacy shawl.

'Where is the nearest, overpriced baby shop?' you ask. 'I must get there quickly before Granny Jenkins comes up with something she has made herself. I can hear her crocheting from here.'

One more worry at this time (apart from all the usual flapping about with the baby because it won't feed/won't stop feeding/gets the hiccups/screams all night – you know the story) is the question of whether or not the proud father videotaped the birth for posterity. Because if he did, he might bring it round to show you one evening. You might like to keep a bucket of hot, soapy water ready for that eventuality.

CHAPTER NINE

WHAT'S THE POINT OF GRANDCHILDREN?

My friend says that she doesn't see the point of grandchildren. She's the one who fainted at the sight of her first grandchild. She said the next one seemed all right, but when she went to its first birthday party, it bit her.

'They're a catalyst,' I told her. 'Imagine a baby that weighs in at about eight pounds: that's like a bomb packed with eight pounds of explosive going off in the family home at regular intervals. Things will never be the same again.'

How truly I spoke.

All new babies like to have one good crying session (I'm talking hours here) for no reason on God's earth. Obviously this is your cue to go home. You have worries of your own to consider.

What if you don't like this baby? It's a possibility, isn't it? If you didn't like the baby you would have to pretend that you did, I suppose, which would mean living a lie until you breathed your last breath. The alternative, of course, would involve some brutal honesty, which carries with it the risk of getting pointed and hissed at in the street for ever more.

Look on the bright side. Maybe it will improve with age. Another friend of mine says the rule is: 'Ugly in cradle; beauty at table'. (She was talking about girls, of course. I don't know what happens to ugly boys.) But whatever it looks like, you are going to have to bond with that baby. Bonding? How do you do that?

As a general rule, I don't like babies. I am not a peerer into prams. But every baby has to be judged as an individual. They may all look quite similar at first glance, but closer inspection reveals subtle shadings of difference.

Does it seem that your grandchild has a more pleasing arrangement of features than the baby in the next cot? Yes, it does. Well, I never. This is one of nature's genuine miracles. Remember how beautiful your own babies were? Now it seems to have happened again.

What's the Point of Grandchildren?

You may be invited to pick the baby up and hold it. You may not really want to do this, but it is meant to be a privilege, so get on with it. Even if it is one of those modern, huge ones, you're not really likely to drop it, are you? But if you find yourself holding the baby, do sit down. If you try to walk about with your arms full of well-wrapped baby, you will find that you can't see where you're going. Whoops! Who left that toy rabbit on the floor?

There is another reason for this over-cautious approach that I hardly like to mention. You are a grandmother now and grandmothers are, by definition, not as clever as parents.

You can see the baby's mother and father watching you nervously. They don't trust you. You, who reared your children single-handedly (well, almost). You, who caught them EVERY TIME they fell downstairs or out of the pantry window. How things change . . .

You are going to have to get used to the idea of stepping gracefully aside. Your children are the master race now. Your daughter's opinions will be sought by worthy people on every subject as soon as she starts swanning around with a pram. As long as she remembers to start every sentence with 'Speaking as a mother . . .' her credentials will not be challenged.

Your thoughts and feelings are never challenged either, but that is because nobody ever asks you what you think. All that wisdom borne so lightly! All that priceless knowledge stored away, never to be enquired upon. Such a waste! But you Must resist the temptation to have an opinion because this might be misinterpreted as 'interfering'.

Interfering is an Unforgivable Sin when you are a grandmother. Interfering grandmothers are regarded in much the same way as warty old women with black cats were in the olden days.

Talking of warty old women, what about your own grandmothers? Thinking back, what do you remember of them? Well, to be honest, all you can remember is how awesomely old they were. They would hover uncertainly on the edges of family gatherings like visiting spirits, not quite part of anything that was going on.

Their child-rearing methods consisted mainly, so you have been told, of leaving their babies in a pram in the garden for most of the day – whatever the weather. No role models there, then.

In the shaky, tumultuous time that follows the birth of a baby, you can rely on no one to stick up for you. It's every relative for himself. You have no allies. ONLY YOU CAN IMPRINT YOURSELF ON THAT CHILD'S MIND AS THE BRINGER OF MIRTH AND CHOCOLATE. Decide now how you wish the baby to think of you, and start acting the part at once. (To become the lovely person you plan to be might take a little practice.)

Experts on children's behaviour keep changing their minds about how soon babies can identify people. No doubt it is sooner than anyone thinks. Get started. You don't want to get muddled up with Granny Jenkins, do you?

'Whose nose is that?' discussions will dominate cot-side visits. Just remember that laying claim to that nose or to the baby's very fine eyebrows will endear you to no one. The parents must be allowed to believe that *they* have given their baby its finest features. Never take sides should any dispute arise about whose genes went where. However blindingly obvious it might be that the baby's delicate violin-player's fingers come from your side of the family, try not to mention it.

CHAPTER TEN

SHOULD GRANDFATHERS BE ALLOWED A LOOK-IN?

Grandfathers are useful for taking videos of the new baby in family groups, with you at the centre.

Should Grandfathers Be Allowed a Look-In?

(I have left a space here in case you can think of anything else to be said for grandfathers.)

CHAPTER ELEVEN

THE FUTURE

It's time to celebrate – and when you feel better, to begin to think about all the good things that having a grandchild will mean. You must remember to tell that friend of yours who doesn't see the point of grandchildren about all the great things that she can look forward to: having someone to take to the pantomime is good.

Not All Grannies Knit

It really is true, you will discover to your delight, that there can be a strong bond between grandmothers and grandchildren. Interests and enthusiasms often skip a generation, giving you and your grandchild much more in common than you might have had with your own children.

You may find that at last there is someone in the family with EXACTLY your sense of humour. And, in time, someone who could well share your passion for bees or Shakespeare or rock climbing.

In the meantime, you can look forward to the arrival of shaky messages and bright, urgent drawings, hot from the inky fingers of the grandchild. They are better than anything else the postman ever brings. Time to buy yourself a scrapbook because they will be good to look back on later:

'And what is this one? It looks like a beetroot on a stick?'

'That's Mum in her dressing gown. Can't you see?'

'Oh, now you mention it . . .'

The Future

Not All Grannies Knit

Outings together are full of unexpected pleasures. That Old Boot who lives next door smiles at you for the first time in her life. The saleswomen in elegantly empty shops watch indulgently while you stand outside laughing at their window displays. Waitresses and waiters race each other to bring that second helping of chocolate pudding to your table. You know perfectly well that the child's mother would not approve. But who is going to tell her? Not you or your little co-conspirator, that's for sure.

As well as the question 'Why?', grandchildren also bring the question 'Why not?' into your life. You will be amazed at how often, when you consider the question carefully, there is no reason why not. No good reason anyway. This is wonderfully liberating. As far as food is concerned this means that you can dye your mashed potatoes any colour you like, and if you want to try putting icing on a jelly, there's no need to feel inhibited about it.

Young minds are tireless seekers after truth. Unfortunately, they sometimes seek truth a bit too close to home, as in 'What are you drinking?', 'Are you going bald?' or 'What does "bastard" mean?'

Then there are the surprising phone calls:

You: 'Hello?'

GRANDCHILD: 'I've been sick in a bucket.'

And should a grandchild come to stay one day, you can do things your own way. In your own house, your own rules apply as they have always done. Just make sure that he or she is not still helping the dog to dig a hole in the flowerbed when your daughter comes to pick up her little treasure.

You will learn to admire and envy your grandchild's gift of selective hearing. Like dogs they can hear a sweet paper unwrapping or a biscuit tin lid coming off from gardens away, but should a parent be banging on about something boring, not a word gets through.

CHAPTER TWELVE

CHRISTMAS WILL NEVER BE THE SAME AGAIN

A word of warning for the future – spending Christmas with older grandchildren can be unexpectedly tricky. Why this should be is a mystery, but for some reason there is something irresistibly funny about accident-prone Grannies at Christmas.

In my own family 'The Year The Tree Fell On Granny' is remembered with particular pleasure. Another time, all the silver charms from the Christmas pudding were accounted for except one. It had to be Granny who had eaten the old Penny Farthing Bicycle by mistake. Unable to contain our laughter, we then had to decide whether to tell her or not. No, we didn't.

Not All Grannies Knit

One more word of warning. Because Christmas is a time for families, grandmothers are very often invited to join the family at that time, especially if they live a long way away. (You can see them all over the country, driving urgently up and down motorways, and hauling suitcases bigger than themselves onto buses and trains.) So excited to be asked. So happy. But when they walk through the front door, who is the first person they set eyes on? Why, it's the Other Granny . . .

Yes, *she's* there too. It's FAMILY TIME, you see. But the worst of it is that Other Granny has inflexible rules about How Christmas Should Be Done, which do not chime in with the proper way of doing things at all. This, I hardly need to tell you, is a recipe for disaster.

Must 'Goodwill to all Men' include other grannies, do you suppose? I don't think so. However festive the season, it is hard to forgive grannies who, for instance, hijack the turkey on Christmas Eve and stuff it with something from an old family recipe that tastes (you discover the next day) like boiled bedsocks. And who put plastic holly on the Christmas pud? Plastic holly smells awful when it catches fire, although it does make a jolly blaze.

Granny Jenkins spares herself no effort – unfortunately. Knitting a nativity scene for the grandchildren is no problem: so we have the Holy Family with crib, shepherds with sheep, Magi with gifts, oxen and asses, and a hen – where did that come from? You would think after all that she might relax, but no.

If there are enough children around she will arrange for them to put on a little play to entertain the grown-ups, which is an ordeal for everyone – especially the children. Then carols must be sung, which is worse for the adults because they don't know the words and are expected to do those high bits where the descant soars off on its own. Humiliation awaits those who attempt this, especially after a heavy lunch and Granny Jenkins's 'special stuffing'.

A Family at Christmas is a dangerous place for a Grandmother to be. Safest to go home as soon as you have delivered the loot. Father Christmas was no fool.

A carol:

> *'It's Christmastide*
> *So run and hide*
> *Lest Granny should be*
> *Mortified.'*

But let future horrors take care of themselves if and when the time comes. If the need arose, you could always develop a silvery laugh to drown out the tinkling crash of the tree falling on you and the fizz of fusing fairy lights. And to show what a good sport you are of course.

For the time being, and for the next few years, you can once again play your part in the miraculous conspiracy that takes place every Christmas. You can join in the anticipation as the Advent calendar counts down the days, and marvel to yourself how easy it is for young children to take flying reindeer and fat old men whizzing up and down chimneys in their stride.

Buying Christmas and birthday presents is one of the treats of grandparenting, so don't let anyone interfere. Take no notice whatever of the mother's earnest requests for educational aids. Children can spot immediately any attempt to teach them by stealth. They will turn their faces away in disgust.

In spite of the annoying presence of some of the other adults, and the fact that you realize too late that the gift you bought for Granny Jenkins is far too good for her, it is still well worth spending some time at Christmas with your grandchild if you can. On Christmas Eve you don't need snow or heavenly choirs or cattle kneeling down at midnight; you just need a small child (preferably in pyjamas) airborne with excitement and delight.

CHAPTER THIRTEEN

BALLOONS AND OTHER HIDDEN HORRORS

I must admit that there is one big disadvantage to having grandchildren around. BALLOONS!

People give children balloons for any old reason these days – just for ordering a pizza or having their hair cut. I wish they wouldn't. The balloons either whizz off into deep space or they explode. (Children's parties should always be avoided for this very reason.)

Out shopping you see a child coming towards you with a loaded balloon and bang goes your peace of mind. Within the family my dislike of sudden, loud noises is well known, so the children try to win me round by giving names to their balloons.

IT DOESN'T WORK. Myfanwy, going off like a mortar bomb without any warning, still has me clawing at the wall. (I think the clawing must be a primitive urge to climb out of danger – doubtless inherited from some monkey ancestor.)

Games of Boo! can be tricky too. Only play this game when the children are very young and you know perfectly well where they are hiding. Older children will either jump out on you unexpectedly and frighten you half to death, or will not be where you thought they were and frighten you half to death for a quite different reason:

YOU (*in a panic*): 'Where are you? I'll give you a hundred pounds if you come out now!'

CHILD (*instantly*): 'Here I am.'

CHAPTER FOURTEEN

LOOK OUT, THERE'S A BABY ABOUT

There is a lot of wishful thinking involved in the momentous occasion that is Baby's First Word. The confusion is natural because it is difficult to be sure what the baby said. You may think you heard: 'Burble, burble. How lucky I am to have a grandmother like you. Burble, burble . . .' but you can't be sure.

The trouble with babies is that they don't speak clearly. I suppose it must be because they don't have enough teeth, but it's still very irritating. Shouting 'SAY THAT AGAIN' doesn't work unfortunately.

I think it is best, after all, to let the parents persuade themselves that it was 'Mama' or 'Dada' that came out first. After all, they have been coaching the child from day one. Indeed you have heard them being quite shameless about it, as if it was a parrot rather than a baby they were talking to.

As babies gradually develop during their first months, you would be wise to look to your personal safety and the even tenor of your mind when dealing with them.

My Unfortunate Friend was persuaded (against her better judgement, of course) to babysit for half an hour one afternoon. She left the baby (who was a few months old) lying fast asleep on a blanket in the middle of the floor while she went into the kitchen to make herself a sandwich. When she came back, the baby was gone.

'That's funny', she thought, and a succession of frightening images passed through her mind:

Her daughter screaming the house down and vowing never to speak to her again.

A judge in a black cap sentencing her to ten years' hard labour for criminal negligence.

A lynch mob made up of her closest friends coming to find her and stringing her up from the nearest lamp post.

It turned out that the baby had rolled under the sofa while she was out of the room.

'I didn't know they ROLLED!' she wailed, still upset when she rang me up later that day.

Apart from the odd practical joke, babies have other ways of making you suffer. People on the whole are much too ready to be taken in by a baby's innocent expression and goofy smile.

Have you ever tried to get a baby into a pushchair when it didn't want to go? It's like trying to get a short plank to sit down. This is a particularly effective tactic from the baby's point of view when you are in a hurry trying to get on or off a bus or a train.

Remember to stay on your toes. A rather absent-minded friend of mine was walking through his kitchen one day, minding his own business, when he was hit between the eyes by a pot of yogurt. Whence, he asked himself, came the offending yogurt? On investigation he found that his tiny granddaughter was in the room, in her highchair, having breakfast. 'I can't say for sure it was her,' he told me. 'But whoever it was, their aim was first class.'

'Cave infantem!' he wrote, as he summed up the day's events in his journal that night.

CHAPTER FIFTEEN

A LAST WORD

Not All Grannies Knit

Firstly, try not to knit.

It isn't a good idea to keep photographs of the children in your wallet. Young sales assistants will spot them and then they will patronize you.

Never criticize any member of the grandchild's family (especially Granny Jenkins) in the child's hearing. Remember what a lovely person you decided to pretend to be. Stick to it.

Resign yourself to the fact that you are now labelled for life.
If you have a set-to with a burglar the newspaper will say:
'Grandmother stuns thief with gin bottle.' If you win the Nobel
Peace Prize, it will be: 'Grandmother (aged fifty-four) says,
"It was nothing really."'

A Last Word

In time there may be more grandchildren. Some people like to boast about how many grandchildren they have. As you are not responsible for how many of them there are, you can't brag about it either, I'm afraid. Just make a point of trying to remember their names.

A carload of grandchildren on their way over for a visit calls for military-style planning. Before they arrive, make sure that those precious framed photographs you were given for Christmas are up on the walls. Check that every child appears in a photograph somewhere. If you've missed anyone out, their mother will notice before you've even closed the front door.

As Shakespeare said about something completely different: 'Some are born grandmothers; some achieve grandmotherhood and some have grandmotherhood thrust upon them.' Whichever way it happened to you, these new members of the family can transform your life for the better if you let them.

Their clear, uncomplicated point of view can sluice out your mind like a bracing mouthwash, making your hair stand on end and bringing tears to your eyes. Grown-up stuffiness has nowhere to hide.

Be thankful. Be-sotted.

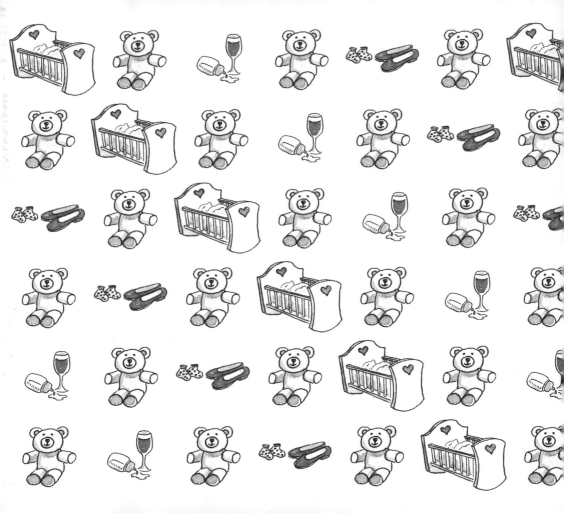